Laughter Was Created for Days Like This

Prayers, Chuckles & Reminders That God Really Has Things Under Control

Inspired by Faith

Laughter Was Created for Days Like This
©Product Concept Mfg., Inc.

Laughter Was Created for Days Like This
ISBN 978-0-9843328-9-2

Published by Product Concept Mfg., Inc.
2175 N. Academy Circle #200, Colorado Springs, CO 80909

All scripture quotations are from the King James version
of the Bible unless otherwise noted.

Scriptures taken from the Holy Bible,
New International Version®, NIV®.
Copyright © 1973, 1978, 1984 by Biblica, Inc.™
Used by permission of Zondervan.
All rights reserved worldwide.
www.zondervan.com

Sayings not having a credit listed are contributed by writers
for Product Concept Mfg., Inc. or in a rare case,
the author is unknown.

Laughter
Was Created
for Days
Like This

Chapter 1

Who Me, stressed???

Call upon me in the day of trouble:
I will deliver thee.
—*Psalm 50:15*

Stress is when you wake up screaming,
then realize you haven't even fallen asleep yet!

Too much on your calendar?
Just take things one at a time.
God did. Remember?
On the first day, He divided
the light and the darkness,
and on the second day...

*When everything seems to be going against you,
remember that the airplane takes off
against the wind, not with it.
—Henry Ford*

Good-humor makes all things tolerable.
—Henry Ward Beecher

Mountains are removed by
first shoveling away the small stones.

I know God will not
give me anything I can't handle.
I just wish that He didn't trust me so much.
—Mother Teresa

You're way too busy
if you never have time to...

~ do something you really enjoy

~ eat a meal with your family

~ listen to others

~ watch the clouds roll by

~ take a nap

~ get in touch with friends

~ pet an animal

~ read a book or a magazine

~ discover something new

~ laugh

~ pray

If you're struggling
to keep an even keel,
Let Him take over the oars
for a while.

*Present opportunities are neglected,
and attainable good is slighted,
by minds busied in extensive ranges
and intent upon future advantages.
—Samuel Johnson*

Even when things are going wrong,
keep going right.

Nothing To Do?

One Sunday, Pastor's sermon focused on how the children of Israel left Egypt and how they wandered in the desert for 40 years. On the way home from church, Mom asked Tommy if he remembered what Pastor had talked about. "Sure," Tommy replied. "He talked about the children of Israel and everything they did. What I wonder is, what were the grown-ups doing all this time?"

The only thing worse
than hearing the alarm clock in the morning
is not hearing it.

Sometimes you get the best view of the
stars when everything around you has
fallen down.

The first proof of a well-ordered mind is to
be able to pause and linger within itself.
—*Seneca*

If you. . .

. . .find it hard to make a joyful noise
today, talk to the Song Leader.

. . . find you have a long row to hoe
today, remember that
He's still in charge of the garden.

. . .can't thank God for what you have,
thank Him for what you have escaped.

Ambition compels us to work
ourselves to death in order to live.

*One cannot collect
all the beautiful shells on the beach.*
—Anne Morrow Lindbergh

Serenity is not
the absence of activity,
but the presence of God
in everything you do.

Never put off until tomorrow
what you can do today,
because if you enjoy it today,
you can do it again tomorrow.

If you can keep your head
when all about you are losing theirs…
you probably don't understand the issues.

Life wastes itself
while we are preparing to live.
—Ralph Waldo Emerson

God is everywhere. . .
even at your wit's end.

Perhaps some day it will be pleasant to
remember even this.
—Virgil

In difficult and hopeless situations
the boldest plans are the safest.
—Titus Livy

*Start by doing what's necessary,
then what's possible,
and suddenly you are doing
the impossible.*
—St. Francis of Assisi

When God pilots your ship,
you need never fear storms.

*Keep cool: it will all be one a hundred
years hence.*
—Ralph Waldo Emerson

*If we had no winter, the spring
would not be so pleasant; if we did
not sometimes taste of adversity,
prosperity would not be so welcome.*
—Anne Bradstreet

God never promised to take you
out of your problems, but He did
promise to take you through them.

God cares about every
little bitty, teeny tiny, itsy bitsy
thing in your day.

Everything is changing;
God alone is changeless.
—Teresa of Avila

Remember that there is nothing stable in human affairs; therefore avoid undue elation in prosperity, or undue depression in adversity.
—Socrates

When you have got an elephant by the hind legs and he is trying to run away, it's best to let him run.
—Abraham Lincoln

Chapter 2

Help is just a prayer away!

Pray without ceasing.
— 1 Thessalonians 5:17

Pray as if everything depended on
God, and work as
if everything depended on you.

A problem not worth
praying about is not worth
worrying about.

God loves
the sound of your voice –
talk to Him every day.

It's true: knees bent in
prayer stand up straighter.

God loves to get knee-mail.

More is accomplished by
folding the hands than by wringing them.

Sound Familiar?

Dear God...

...Your will be done,
but I hope You realize that
I'll never be happy unless
I get exactly what I want.

...I have sinned,
but let me tell You who's to blame.

...give me patience,
Lord, and give it to me now!

...help me be more tolerant
of the opinions of others,
even though they're dead wrong.

...I lay my future in Your hands,
Lord, and here's what needs to happen.

...take away these troubles,
Lord, because I've already learned everything
I need to know from the experience.

...help me be less of a perfectionist, Lord,
and help me do it exactly right.

Dr. God has a prescription for stress—it's called prayer.

If you don't pray when the sun shines, you won't know how when the clouds come.

Thank God for all the times you *didn't* get what you prayed for!

There's dial-a-prayer for atheists – you call the number, and nobody answers!

Joy and thankfulness are
the secret ingredients to all
successful prayer.

More tears are shed over
answered prayers than
unanswered ones.
—Teresa of Avila

Ask for His gifts,
but trust Him to send you
the right size and color.

Prayer as a means
to effect a private end
is meanness and theft.
It supposes dualism and not unity
in nature and consciousness.
As soon as the man is
one with God,
he will not beg.
He will then see
prayer in all action.
—Ralph Waldo Emerson

You don't have to worry about falling
if you're down on your knees.

*Our prayers should be burning words
coming forth from the furnace
of a heart filled with love.
—Mother Teresa*

God tells us to burden Him
with whatever burdens us.

Rescued!

A homeowner stood on the roof of his house as flood waters inched up to the eaves. "Lord, help me," he cried to the heavens.

A neighbor on a raft paddled near and yelled, "Climb aboard!"

"No, thank you," shouted the homeowner, waving him away. "I've prayed for the Lord to help me."

In a few minutes, a rescue boat pulled up and a man yelled, "Jump in!" But the homeowner repeated his answer and shooed the rescue boat away.

The homeowner continued to pray and the water continued to rise. Then a helicopter

appeared over the horizon and swooped straight toward the man on the roof. The copter hovered, a rope dropped out, and the copter pilot shouted through a bullhorn, "We're here to help—hold on to the rope and we'll pull you up!" But the man replied, "I've prayed for the Lord to help me, so you don't need to!"

The homeowner perished in the flood. In heaven, he approached the Lord. "I prayed to You, so why didn't You help me when I called on You?" he demanded.

"My dear man," the Lord replied, "I sent you a raft, a boat, and a helicopter. Why didn't you accept My help?"

God's ear lies close to the
believer's lip.

To pray...is to desire;
but it is to desire what God
would have us desire.
—Francois Fenelon

We, ignorant of ourselves, beg
often our own harms, which the
wise powers deny us for our good.
—William Shakespeare

*In prayer it is better to have a heart
without words than words without
a heart.*
—John Bunyan

*From silly devotions and from
sour-faced saints, good Lord,
deliver us!*
—Teresa of Avila

7 days without prayer
makes 1 weak.

There is a vast difference between
saying prayers and praying.

All prayers are answered if
we are willing to admit that
sometimes the answer is "no."

Remember, there's nothing too big or too small to share with your Heavenly Father.

Prayer is wireless access to God – no matter where you are.

The most powerful position you can take is on your knees.

Without the incense of heartfelt prayer,
even the greatest of cathedrals is dead.

When the knees are not
often bent, the feet do slide.

Do not pray by heart, but with heart.

*I have been driven many
times to my knees by the
overwhelming conviction that
I had nowhere else to go.
—Abraham Lincoln*

When we start
kneeling down,
things start looking up.

*Satan trembles when he sees the
weakest saint upon his knees.
—William Cowper*

Chapter 3

Ooops!

*As far as the east is from the west, so far has
he removed our transgressions from us.
—Psalm 103:12 NIV*

Moses started out life as a
basket case, but the Lord made
something of him anyway.

An embarrassing moment
is spitting out a car window
when it's not open.

If your mind goes blank,
be sure to turn off the sound.

When feeling sheepish,
turn to the Shepherd.

*Our bravest and best lessons
are not learned through success, but
through misadventure.*
—Amos B. Alcott

*It is never too late
to be what you might have been.*
—George Eliot

*Have patience with all things, but
chiefly have patience with yourself.
Do not lose courage
in considering your
own imperfections, but instantly set
about remedying them—
every day begin the task anew.*
—Francis de Sales

Enjoy today and don't waste it grieving over a bad yesterday. Who knows? Tomorrow may be even worse!

The Lord is my Shepherd, even when I'm a ba-a-a-ad sheep.

Forbidden fruit causes many jams.

Do not be too timid and squeamish about your actions. All life is an experiment. The more experiments you make the better. What if they are a little coarse, and you may get your coat soiled or torn? What if you do fail, and get fairly rolled in the dirt once or twice? Up again, you shall nevermore be so afraid of a tumble.
—Ralph Waldo Emerson

Your greatest triumphs are
not in winning, but in rising
again after every fall.

*If you hear that someone is
speaking ill of you, instead of
trying to defend yourself you
should say: "He obviously does
not know me very well, since
there are so many other faults
he could have mentioned."*
—*Epictetus*

Exercise daily –
run from sin
and walk with God.

I don't like people who have never fallen or stumbled. Their virtue is lifeless and it isn't of much value. Life hasn't revealed its beauty to them.
—Boris Pasternak

It is human to err, but it is devilish to remain willfully in error.
—Augustine

If you're headed in the wrong
direction on the highway of life,
God allows U-turns.

*God moves in a mysterious way
His wonders to perform.*
—William Cowper

*Only he who does nothing
makes no mistakes.*
—French Proverb

Do the math:
     1 cross
   + 3 nails
   _____
   = 4 given

Chapter 4

Hey, Lord, can you ease up just a little?

Cast all your anxiety on him
because he cares for you.
—1 Peter 5:7 NIV

Lose weight fast:
shed your burdens!

Worry is one thing
you should never recycle.

*Life consists of what a man is
thinking of all day.*
–Ralph Waldo Emerson

*The pain passes,
but the beauty remains.*
—Pierre-Auguste Renoir

When the storms of life rock your
boat, call the Captain.

Let Go, Let God

Two friends sat at the kitchen table over coffee. One listened while the other delivered a litany of woes, almost in tears over how much she had to bear. When at last she ran out of words, her understanding friend picked up and held her now-empty coffee cup.

"How much do you think this weighs?" asked the woman.

Bewildered, the burdened woman hazarded a guess of, say, a couple ounces.

"Actually," the woman replied, "it doesn't make any difference how much

the cup weighs. When I pick it up to use it, I can easily handle it. But if I were to pick it up and hold it for an hour, my arm would start to ache. If I held it for three hours, I would be in misery. If I held it until tomorrow, I would probably collapse under the weight of it."

The woman continued. "Our burdens are like that, my friend. We can't carry them 24/7. We need to put them down sometimes and renew our strength… perhaps gain a fresh point of view, or find a good solution. When we pick them up again, they're not quite so heavy, and we often find that we can handle them quite easily."

*If you see ten troubles coming down
the road, you can be sure that nine
will run into the ditch before
they reach you.*
—Calvin Coolidge

Resentments are burdens too heavy
for anyone's shoulders.

*Smooth seas do not
make skillful sailors.*
—African Proverb

Troubles are a lot like babies—
they grow larger
if you nurse them.

In three words I can sum up
everything I've learned about
life: It goes on.
—Robert Frost

Whatever tears one may shed,
in the end one always blows
one's nose.
—Heinrich Heine

The best place to put your troubles is in your pocket—the one with a hole in it.

Worry is paying for trouble you don't have.

Suffering is a very expensive school to attend, but most of us learn in no other way.

If the devil
is knocking at your door,
let Jesus answer.

Pray, and let God worry.
—Martin Luther

Adversities do not
make a man frail.
They show what
sort of man he is.
—Thomas à Kempis

When there's too much
bad news,
catch up on the Good News.

Don't tell God how big your
storm is. Tell the storm how
big your God is.

If you're lost on the
road of life, read The Map.

Here's to the past.
Thank God it's past!

Faith is like a flame that shatters
the darkest night.

If God's in charge of it,
why worry about it?

When at night you cannot
sleep, talk to the Shepherd and
stop counting sheep.

*Earth has no sorrow
that Heaven cannot heal.*
—Thomas Moore

Chapter 5

What's so funny, anyway?

To every thing there is a season…
a time to weep, and a time to laugh.
—Ecclesiastes 3:1, 4

If you want to be happy, be.
—Tolstoy

God put happiness not in the
clouds, but along your path.

Mix a little foolishness with your
serious plans: It's good to be silly
at the right moment.
—Horace

For a free face-lift, smile.

When you can laugh at yourself, you're never at a loss for humor.

One should take good care not to grow too wise for so great a pleasure of life as laughter.
—Joseph Addison

10 Good Reasons to Smile Through It All

~ Smiling takes less effort than frowning.

~ Smiling relieves stress.

~ Smiling promotes good health.

~ Smiling gives you an instant face lift.

~ Smiling makes your friends wonder what you've been up to.

~ Smiling makes wrinkles
  look like laugh lines.

~ Smiling prompts people to
  smile back.

~ Smiling helps you live longer.

~ Smiling makes you feel as good as
  eating a chocolate bar...
  and has no calories.

And...

Smiling is simply more fun!

True happiness may be sought, thought,
or caught—but never bought.

A good laugh is like manure to a
farmer—it doesn't do any good
until you spread it around.

The robbed that smiles,
steals something from the thief.
–William Shakespeare

Earth's crammed with heaven.
—Elizabeth Barrett Browning

If you want to find out how rich you are,
count all the things you have
that money can't buy.

Finally, brothers, whatever is true,
whatever is noble, whatever is right,
whatever is pure, whatever is lovely,
whatever is admirable—
if anything is excellent or praiseworthy—
think about such things.
–Philippians 4:8 NIV

—Just Asking

A father was reading a Bible story to his young son. Dad read, "God told Lot to take his wife and flee the city, but Lot's wife looked back and was turned into a pillar of salt."

"Wow!" his son exclaimed. "But Dad, what happened to the flea?"

No matter how grouchy
you're feeling,
You'll find the smile
more or less healing.
It grows in a wreath
All around the front teeth—
Thus preserving the face
from congealing.
—Anthony Euwer

A giggle is
God's grace in Motion.

*Laughter is the closest thing to the
grace of God.*
—Karl Barth

*Cheerfulness keeps up a kind of
daylight in the mind, and fills it with
a steady and perpetual serenity.*
—Joseph Addison

*Laughter is the sun that drives winter
from the human face.*
—Victor Hugo

Enjoy yourself.
These are the "good old days"
you're going to miss in the years ahead.

*The sign of wisdom
is a continual cheerfulness.*
—French proverb

Show me an optimist,
and I'll show you a happy-condriac.

A person without a sense of
humor is like a wagon without
springs – jolted by every pebble
in the road.
—Henry Ward Beecher

*He who tickles himself
may laugh when he pleases.
–Proverb*

*The best thing one can do when it's
raining is to let it rain.*
—Henry Wadsworth Longfellow

Even if there's nothing to laugh
at, laugh on credit.

*Mirth is like a flash of lightning that
breaks through a gloom of clouds
and glitters for a moment.*
—Joseph Addison

He who laughs, lasts.

The foolish seek happiness over the horizon. The wise find it under their feet.

Chapter 6

Trying to walk the walk.

Remember the Sabbath day,
to keep it holy.
—Exodus 20:8

The trouble with trouble is that it always starts out like fun.

God wrote only one Book.
Don't you think
you should read it?

Any idiot can face a crisis—
it's this day-to-day living that
wears you out.
–Anton Chekhov

There is nothing either good or
bad, but thinking makes it so.
–William Shakespeare

*How many legs does a dog have if
you call the tail a leg? Four. Calling
a tail a leg doesn't make it a leg.*
—*Abraham Lincoln*

*When you want to fool the world,
tell the truth.*
—*Bismarck*

Some of the people who say
"Our Father" on Sundays
go around the rest of the week acting
as if they were orphans.

Faith is a sounder guide than reason.
Reason can only go so far,
but faith has no limits.
—Blaise Pascal

The best preparation
for tomorrow
is the right use of today.

Stop, Thief!

A woman, returning home from church one Sunday, came face-to-face with a burglar in her house. "Acts 2:38!" she yelled. "Turn from your sin!"

The burglar froze, and the woman called the police, who came to the home immediately.

As the burglar was being handcuffed, the woman told the officer that she had stopped him by citing a Bible verse.

"A Bible verse!" protested the burglar. "Heck no! She told me she had an ax and two .38s!"

Don't opt for fast food
when God is serving soul food.

How come I can't wait to call
my friends...but wait until
Sunday to call my Friend?

If life were a
do-it-yourself project,
God would not have left
His Instruction Book.

*Seek not to understand that thou mayest believe,
but believe that thou mayest understand.*
—Augustine

If life is a comedy to him who thinks,
and a tragedy to him who feels,
it is a victory to him who believes.

*Faith is a living and unshakable confidence,
a belief in the grace of God so assured that a man
would die a thousand deaths for its sake.*
—Martin Luther

I'll Get There!

A little girl, late for Sunday school, was running as fast as she could toward church. As she ran, she prayed, "Dear Jesus, please don't make me late for Sunday school." Just as she was within sight of the church, she tripped and fell, bruising her knee and dirtying her clothes. Undaunted, the little girl got up and started running again, this time praying, "Dear Jesus, please don't make me late for Sunday school, but please don't push me, either."

Forgive your enemies —
it messes with their minds.

Have courage for the great
sorrows of life and patience for
the small ones; and when you
have laboriously accomplished
your daily task, go to sleep in
peace. God is awake.
—Victor Hugo

The Holy Spirit expects spiritual
fruit, not religious nuts.

He who loses wealth loses much.
He who loses a friend loses more;
but he that loses his courage loses all.
—Miguel de Cervantes

Your words are windows
to your mind and heart.

Everything that is done in the world is
done by hope.
—Martin Luther

Heaven Is My Home

The Sunday school teacher asked her
class who wanted to go to heaven.
All hands shot up except one.
"Why don't you want to go to
heaven, Jackie?" the teacher asked.
"I'd like to go," Jackie replied,
"but my mom told me to come
straight home today."

I think one's feelings waste themselves in words; they ought all to be distilled into actions, and into actions which bring results.
—Florence Nightingale

Get your exercise today!
Walk with the Lord.

If we did all the things we are capable of doing, we would literally astound ourselves.
—Thomas Edison

*A humble knowledge of oneself is
a surer road to God than a deep
searching of the sciences.*
—Thomas à Kempis

*Before me, even as behind,
God is, and all is well.*
—John Greenleaf Whittier

Affirmation

The light of God surrounds me,

The love of God enfolds me,

The power of God protects me,

The Presence of God watches over me.

Wherever I am, God is.

If you desire direction from God, be prepared
to accept correction from God.

Light tomorrow with today!
—Elizabeth Barrett Browning

Walk with the wise and be
wise; mix with the stupid
and be misled.

Happy Travels

A minister boarded an airplane and sat down. As the plane taxied out onto the runway and prepared for take-off, the clergyman became visibly panic-stricken. The woman sitting next to him looked over and said, "Now Pastor, I'm surprised. You of all people should know that God is with you."

"Yes," the ashen-faced minister replied, "but remember He said: *Lo*, I am with you always."

God never asks you to search for Him,
because He has found you first.

Enjoy the little things—after all,
there are so many of them!

God cares about the big things, the small
things, and all things in between.

Too many churchgoers are singing
"Standing on the Promises" when all
they are doing is sitting on the premises.

Action is eloquence.
—William Shakespeare

Opportunity is missed by most people
because it is dressed in overalls
and looks like work.
—Thomas Edison

Avoid truth decay—
brush up on the Bible daily.

Truth is such a rare thing,
it is delightful to tell it.
—Emily Dickinson

Make happy those
who are near,
and those who are far
will come.

You cannot teach a man
anything; you can only help
him to find it within himself.
—Galileo

We know the truth, not only by
the reason, but also by the heart.
—Blaise Pascal

Your friends are like the buttons
on an elevator.
They can take you
either up or down.

Reputation can be made
in a moment, but character
takes a lifetime.

*You can tell the character
of every man when you see
how he receives praise.*
—Seneca

Chapter 7

It's got to get better!

*I press toward the mark for the prize of the
high calling of God in Christ Jesus.*
—Philippians 3:14

Let nothing disturb you,
nothing frighten you;
all things are passing;
God never changes.
—Teresa of Avila

Though the grass may look
greener on the other side,
it still has to be mowed.

Hope is itself a species of
happiness, and, perhaps,
the chief happiness which
this world affords.
—Samuel Johnson

The bridge between hope and despair
is often a prayer
and a good night's sleep.

We can be so busy listing our
troubles that we forget how to count
our blessings.

You cannot win if you never begin.

Nothing will ever be attempted
if all possible objections must be
first overcome.
–Samuel Johnson

Remember the tea kettle:
even though it's up to its neck in
hot water, it continues to sing.

Hope sees the invisible,
feels the intangible,
and achieves the impossible.

Sorrow looks back.

Worry looks around.

Faith looks up.

God can heal your broken heart,
but He wants you to give Him
all the pieces first.

Hope is the thing with feathers
that perches in the soul
and sings the tune without the words
and never stops... at all.
–Emily Dickinson

*As long as there is one upright
man, as long as there is one
compassionate woman, the
contagion may spread and the
scene is not desolate. Hope is the
one thing left to us in a bad time.*
—*E. B. White*

I resolved to take Fate by the throat
and shake a living out of her.
—Louisa May Alcott

Often one meets his destiny in the
road he took to avoid it.
—French proverb

*A hero is no braver than an
ordinary man, but he is brave
five minutes longer.
–Ralph Waldo Emerson*

*Fortune favors the bold.
-Virgil*

Do the thing you fear,
and you are certain to see the
death of fear.

Courage is often just ignorance
of the facts.

An acorn is not an oak tree when it is sprouted. It must go through long summers and fierce winters; it has to endure all that frost and snow and side-striking winds can bring before it is a full grown oak. So it is with us.
–Henry Ward Beecher

It isn't necessary to stay awake
nights to get through this —
just stay awake days.

Remember: the success of the
woodpecker is due to the fact
he uses his head.

*It is dangerous to abandon one's
self to the luxury of grief;
it deprives one of courage, and
even of the wish for recovery.*
—Henri Amiel

*We can't solve problems by
using the same kind of thinking
we used when we created them.
—Albert Einstein*

Feed your faith, and your
doubts will starve to death.

*A man cannot be comfortable
without his own approval.
—Mark Twain*

Time Flies

An elderly woman was a faithful
churchgoer and an avid reader of the
Bible. In fact, the Bible is all she read.
A friend asked, "Why don't you read
anything other than the Bible?"

"I can't," the woman replied.
"I'm cramming for my finals."

They are able because
they think they are able.
—Virgil

Never bend your head.
Always hold it high.
Look the world straight in the eye.
—Helen Keller

Learn what you are, and be such.
—Pindar

*If one advances confidently in
the direction of his dreams, and
endeavors to live the life which
he has imagined, he will meet
with a success unexpected in
common hours.
—Henry David Thoreau*

New Life

A middle-aged woman had a heart attack and was rushed to the hospital. On her way there, she slipped into a coma and found herself in front of the pearly gates. She asked St. Peter if this was her time, but Peter scanned his book and said no, she had another 35 years to live. Elated, the woman woke up, received treatment, and was released after a short stay in the hospital.

She figured that, if she had another 35 years ahead of her, she would make some changes she had always wanted to make. She had a face-lift, a nose job, a tummy tuck, and

her hair dyed. She bought a whole new wardrobe, and stepped out into the street feeling like a million dollars. Then she was struck by a car and killed.

Back in front of St. Peter, she said, "But you told me I had another 35 years to live!"

"Oh, my mistake," St. Peter said. "I'm sorry, but I didn't recognize you."

Man is the only animal that blushes.
Or needs to.
–Mark Twain

A stitch in time
saves embarrassing exposure.

It is only by forgetting yourself
that you draw near to God.
–Henry David Thoreau

Chapter 8

There are roses in December.

O give thanks unto the LORD;
for he is good.
—Psalm 136:1

It is only with the heart that one
can see rightly; what is essential
is invisible to the eye.
–Antoine de Saint-Exupéry

The day, water, sun, moon, night–
I do not have to purchase these
things with money.
—Plautus

It's not the outlook, but the uplook,
that counts.

A Place for Everything

An administrative assistant,
who had formerly worked at the
Pentagon, came to work as secretary
for a church pastor. The first thing
she did was change the filing
system to SACRED and
TOP SACRED!

To journey hopefully is better than to arrive.

True progress quietly and persistently moves along without notice.
—Francis de Sales

The block of granite which was an obstacle in the pathway of the weak becomes a stepping stone in the pathway of the strong.
—Thomas Carlyle

The optimist keeps his eye on the doughnut, but the pessimist can see only the hole.

A thankful heart is not only the greatest virtue, but the parent of all other virtues.
—Cicero

Be glad of life because it gives you the chance to love, and to work, and to play and to look up at the stars.
—Henry Van Dyke

You have everything when you love everything you have.

My path hitherto has been like a road through a diversified country, now climbing high mountains, then descending into the lowest vales. From the summits I saw the heavens; from the vales I look up at the heights again.
—Henry David Thoreau

Both the optimist and the pessimist
are right, but as different as light is
from darkness.

A single sunbeam is enough
to drive away many shadows.
–St. Francis of Assisi

A pessimist feels bad when he feels
good for fear he'll feel worse
when he feels better.

A wise person cares not for what
he may not have.

We never know the worth
of water until the well is dry.
—English proverb

Let him who has enough
wish for nothing more.
—Horace

...I say grace before the concert and the opera, and grace before the play and pantomime, and grace before I open a book, and grace before sketching, painting, swimming, fencing, boxing, walking, playing, dancing and grace before I dip the pen in the ink.
—G. K. Chesterton

*Nothing is more honorable than a
grateful heart.
—Seneca*

*The person who has stopped being
thankful has fallen asleep in life.
—Robert Louis Stevenson*

A contented mind
is the greatest blessing
a man can enjoy in this world.
—Joseph Addison

Content is the
Philosopher's Stone,
that turns all it touches to gold.
—Benjamin Franklin

Hope is putting faith to
work when doubting would
be easier.

Serenity allows you to
enjoy the scenery when
you're on a detour.

Even though we can't have
everything we want,
we can be thankful we don't get everything
we deserve.

Rest and be thankful.
—William Wordsworth

Chapter 9

It's all in how you look at it!

Unto the pure all things are pure.
—Titus 1:15

*If you are distressed by anything
external, the pain is not due
to the thing itself, but to your
estimate of it; and this you have
the power to revoke
at any moment.*
—Marcus Aurelius

There are two kinds of Christians:
those who complain because God
put thorns on the roses,
and those who praise Him
for putting roses among the thorns.

Growl all day,
and you'll feel dog tired at night.

The best place to find a helping hand
is at the end of your own arm.
—Swedish proverb

Career Goal?

After church one Sunday, Junior announced that he wanted to become a preacher. "Wonderful," his mother replied. "And what made you decide?" "Well," the boy said, "since I have to go to church anyway, I'd rather be standing up and yelling instead of sitting down and listening."

*Not everything that can be counted
counts, and not everything that
counts can be counted.*
—*Albert Einstein*

*It's not what happens to you,
but how you react to it that matters.*
—*Epictetus*

Nothing is miserable
unless you think it is so.
—Boethius

The real voyage of discovery
consists not in seeking new landscapes,
but in having new eyes.
—Marcel Proust

Though life may be understood
by looking backward,
it can be lived only by looking forward.

Faith is daring the soul to go
where the eyes can't see.

*What concerns me is not the way
things are, but rather the way
people think things are.
—Epictetus*

A thought may make
a person a prisoner.

Good News, Bad News

The good news: There is golf in heaven.
It never rains, and you can play as long
as you like!

The bad news: You're scheduled to play
next Tuesday.

The pastor stood up in front of his congregation and told them he had good news and bad news. "The good news," he said, "is that we have money for your new building extension." Everyone cheered. "The bad news is that it's still in your wallets."

"The good news is that the guy who always criticized your sermons has transferred out of this congregation," the deacon informed the pastor. "The bad news is that he's been appointed head of our district."

After Noah landed the ark and let
down the gangplank, the animals
filed out of the craft. Two lions, two
zebras, two tigers...then four gnus!
"Why four gnus?"
Noah's son asked his father.
"Well, son, there's some good gnus
and some bad gnus..."

I have not failed.
I've just found 10,000 ways that won't work.
—Thomas Edison

You can't depend on your eyes when your
imagination is out of focus.
—Mark Twain

A genius is one who shoots at something no
one else can see — and hits it.

To make your dream come true,
you have to stay awake.

Do your duty in all things.
You can not do more.
You should never wish to do less.
—Robert E. Lee

Nothing is easier
than self-deceit.
—Demosthenes

Vision is the
art of seeing things invisible.
—Jonathan Swift

If I had a formula for bypassing trouble, I would not pass it round... Trouble creates a capacity to handle it. I don't say embrace trouble; that's as bad as treating it as an enemy. But I do say, meet it as a friend, for you'll see a lot of it and had better be on speaking terms with it.
—Oliver Wendell Holmes

*A feeble man can see the farms
that are fenced and tilled, the
houses that are built. The strong
man sees the possible houses
and farms. His eye makes estates
as fast as the sun breeds clouds.
—Ralph Waldo Emerson*

Man is what he believes.
—Anton Chekhov

The greatest discovery of my generation
is that human beings can alter their lives
by altering their attitudes of mind."
—William James

*Great men are they who see
that the spiritual is stronger than
any material force, that thoughts
rule the world.*
—*Ralph Waldo Emerson*

*The greater part of our
happiness or misery depends
upon our dispositions,
and not upon our circumstances.*
—*Martha Washington*

Have a God day...

every day!